Hi!

Welcome to this activity book. I hope you have lots of fun with it. And I also hope you will learn some important things that God's book, the Bible, teaches about God, Jesus and you. By the end of this book you should be able to answer this really big question:

Who will be your king?

Before We Begin

When you see this...

...these words are from the Bible.

What is the Bible? The Bible is God's book. God tells us lots of important things in the Bible. (We will learn more about the Bible on pages 26 and 27.)

There are some words the Bible uses that you may not know. If you read a word you're not sure about, see if it's in the Bible Words Dictionary on page 32.

But let's get back to the big question: *Who will be your king?*

To answer it, we need to start at the beginning...

God is the loving king of everything because he made everything in the beginning.

1 God made the whole world and everything in it.

2 So God is in charge of the world.  He is the king.

3 God is not a bossy, selfish king like some human kings.

4 He's kind and loving and good. That's why the world he made is full of good things.

5 God makes people too, and gives us life.

6 That means  is our king.

In the beginning, God created the heavens and the earth.
(Genesis 1:1)

God made
everything.

God made
everyone.

GOD
is the
king of
everything
and everyone.

 Fill this picture with things that God made. Here are some ideas:

God made me and God loves me!

Draw what you look like.

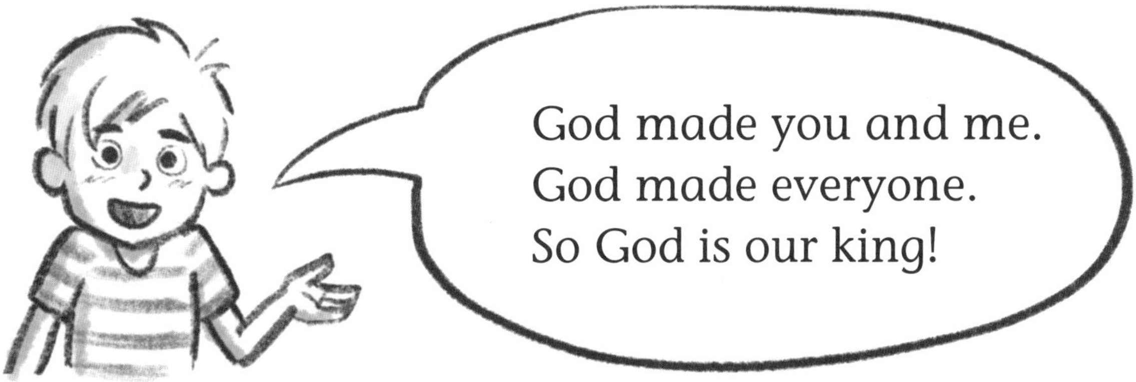

God made you and me.
God made everyone.
So God is our king!

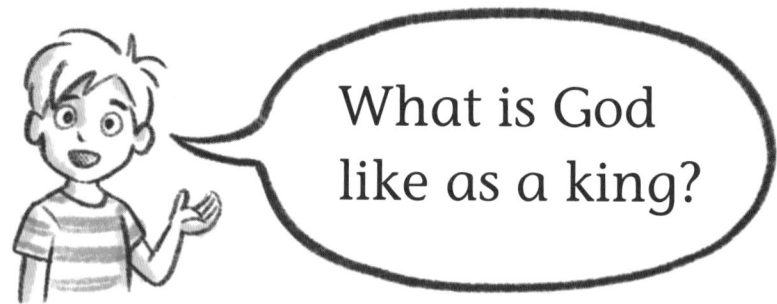

What is God like as a king?

The Bible tells us that

God is a

$\frac{}{11} \frac{}{9} \frac{}{14} \frac{}{4}, \frac{}{12} \frac{}{15} \frac{}{22} \frac{}{9} \frac{}{14} \frac{}{7}$

and $\frac{}{7} \frac{}{15} \frac{}{15} \frac{}{4}$ king!

 Write in the missing words using this code:

A	B	C	D	E	F	G	H	I	J	K	L	M	N	O	P	Q	R	S	T	U	V	W	X	Y	Z
1	2	3	4	5	6	7	8	9	10	11	12	13	14	15	16	17	18	19	20	21	22	23	24	25	26

If God is our loving king, we should read what God says in the Bible, and do what he says. But we don't like doing what God tells us to do...

We say 'No' to God.
We try to be our own king instead.
But we make a big mess of God's good world.

Even though God is the true king, we don't want him to be our king.

We all say 'No' to him by not obeying him as king. We do what we want to do, instead of what God wants us to do. We pretend that we are the king instead of God. This is what the Bible calls 'sin'.

Sin causes lots of problems.

By trying to do things our own way, we hurt each other and make a big mess of God's good world.

THE BIBLE SAYS

No-one is acceptable to God. No-one understands or searches for God. They have all turned away. (Romans 3:10-12)

GOD'S WAY

MY WAY

Sometimes we say 'No' to God by not listening to what he says in his book, the Bible.

THE BIBLE

Sometimes we say 'No' to God by not being kind.

Sometimes we say 'No' to God by doing things we know are wrong.

Please don't step on the flowers

Please don't step on the flowers

Sin (saying NO to God) is pretending I'm king instead of God

 Add some colour to the 'God's way' pictures.

What do you think God is going to do about our sin?

Finish decorating the frame with patterns.

God is the only true king.
He won't let people keep on saying 'No' to him.
God's punishment is that we are shut out of his kingdom forever.

It makes God angry that we don't obey him as king. It also makes him angry that we are selfish, and hurt each other, and make a mess of his world.

God won't let us keep saying 'No' to him. He won't let us keep on pretending to be our own king instead.

One day, God will show everyone that he is the only true king. He will set up a wonderful kingdom that never ends. And on that day, everyone who has been saying 'No' to him will be shut out of his kingdom forever.

THE BIBLE SAYS

We will all die once, and then face judgement.
(Hebrews 9:27)

Finish drawing the crowd.

ONE DAY,
GOD WILL SHOW EVERYONE
THAT HE IS THE

ONE
TRUE
KING!

God is a
kind and loving king,
God is always good.

Quick Quiz

Tick the correct answers.

1. If God is good, that means he…
☐ eats lots of chocolate
☐ is a fast runner
☐ always does the right thing

2. When we do the wrong thing and hurt each other, the right thing for God to do is…
☐ eat lots of chocolate
☐ give us lots of chocolate
☐ punish us
☐ go on a holiday

God is always good. God knows that we deserve to be punished for not obeying him.

See if you can follow the path to finish the sentence.
Colour each path a different colour.

- God is the only true
- God will set up a
- God's kingdom will
- People who keep saying 'No' to God and keep disobeying him

- wonderful kingdom
- never end
- king
- can't be in God's kingdom

We all sin. We keep saying 'No' to God and disobeying him.

So we all deserve to be shut out of God's kingdom forever.

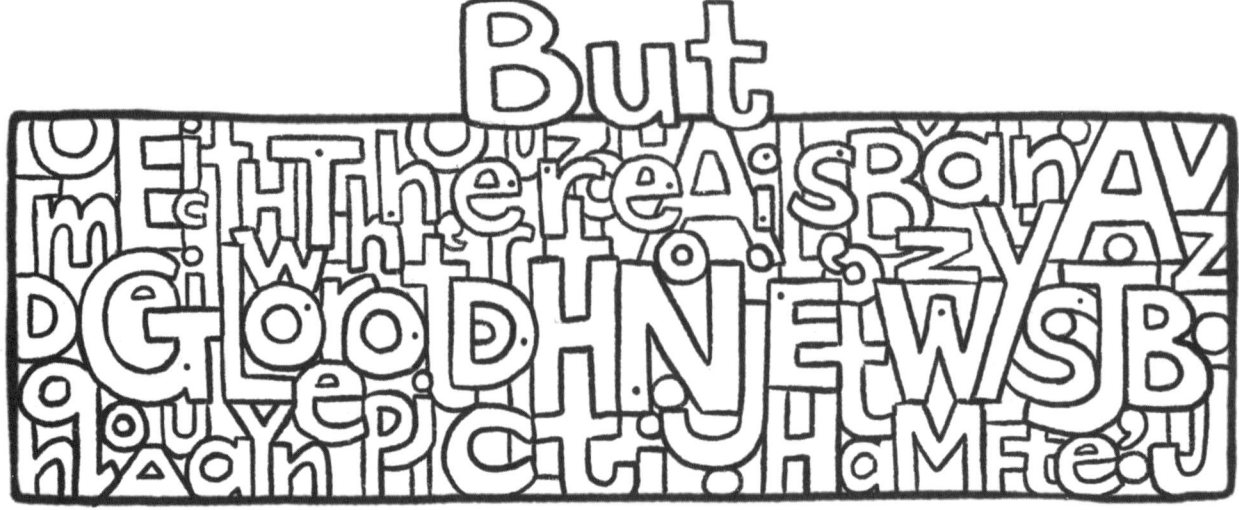

 Colour in the spaces with dots [•] in them.

Because of his love, God sent his Son, Jesus, into the world. Jesus died to take our punishment so that we could be forgiven.

Because he is so loving, God has done something to rescue us from the punishment we deserve.

Many years ago, God sent his own Son, Jesus, into the world. Jesus didn't say 'No' to God. He always did what God wanted him to. And so he didn't deserve to be punished like the rest of us.

But Jesus *was* punished. He was killed on a cross. God loved us so much that he punished his own Son, Jesus, *instead of us.*

This means that we can be forgiven for saying 'No' to God. We can be welcomed into God's wonderful kingdom as his friends.

THE BIBLE SAYS

God loved the world so much that he gave his only Son, so that everyone who trusts in him will have eternal life. (John 3:16)

Think of someone who loves you.
Draw how they show their love to you.

God shows you he loves you in an even more amazing way...

GOD SENT HIS SON
JESUS

Colour in the word 'JESUS', because he is very special!

We sin   We deserve punishment

Jesus didn't sin   Jesus didn't deserve
                          punishment

Jesus took the punishment we deserved instead of us
by dying on a cross.

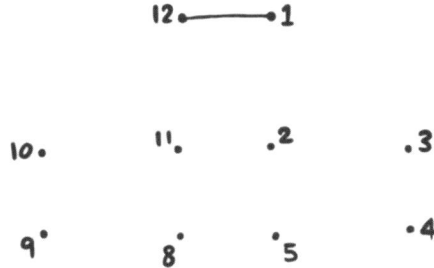

 Join the dots using straight lines.

Because Jesus died on the cross, we can be forgiven for our sin. That means God treats us like we have never sinned—he treats us as his friends.

That's VERY GOOD NEWS!

We can be in God's wonderful kingdom as God's friends.

That's VERY VERY GOOD NEWS!

But there's even more good news...

 Draw some more balloons and colour them in. If you want to, colour in some of the people too.

God brought Jesus back to life again, and made him the king of everything. One day, Jesus will come back.

When people die, we don't see them any more. They stay dead.

But even though Jesus died, God brought him back to life again. And lots of people saw him and even touched him.

Then Jesus left our world and went back to be with God, his Father. And God made Jesus the king of the whole world.

One day, King Jesus will come back to our world. He will punish everyone who is still saying 'No' to God...

...but welcome his forgiven friends into his good kingdom forever.

THE BIBLE SAYS

This Jesus, who was taken up into heaven, will come again in the same way as you saw him go. (Acts 1:11)

Because God brought Jesus back to life again a long time ago, it can be easy to think it's just a made up story. But it's true.

Here is what one of Jesus' friends, named Matthew, wrote down at the time about what happened (this comes from the Bible, in the Gospel of Matthew, chapter 28, verses 1-8).

Mary Magdalene and the other Mary went to see the tomb. Suddenly a strong earthquake struck, and the Lord's angel came down from heaven. He rolled away the stone and sat on it. The angel looked as bright as lightning, and his clothes were white as snow. The guards shook from fear and fell down, as though they were dead.

The angel said to the women, "Don't be afraid! I know you are looking for Jesus, who was nailed to a cross. He isn't here! God has raised him to life, just as Jesus said he would. Come, see the place where his body was lying. Now hurry! Tell his disciples that he has been raised to life and is on his way to Galilee. Go there, and you will see him. That is what I came to tell you."

The women were frightened and yet very happy, as they hurried from the tomb and ran to tell his disciples.

The Bible also tells us that lots of people saw Jesus

ALIVE

For 40 days they saw him, and touched him,
and talked to him, and listened to him.

 Colour in the crowd and see if you can add some more people.

Tick the correct box.

☐ Jesus is a dead king who doesn't matter.

☐ Jesus is our alive-forever king who can help us.

Here's what we've learned so far. Read it and then see if you can find the underlined words in the find-a-word box.

God is king of everything. God is a kind, loving and good king.

Sin (saying 'No' to God) is pretending I am king. But God is the real king.

We all deserve God's punishment.

Jesus took the punishment instead of us. So we can be forgiven.

Jesus is alive!

Jesus is king of everything and everyone!

```
E W M X G L L C L D B Q Y K T F L D P I
C B R S D P T K S P A L M Q N D Q Y G X
Q Q B E F E P I H A R Z Y V O K O Q A P
J K A J Q O V M Y E I E T B V G I P N Z
Y I W Z D E S E R V E Q T H S R X E Q S
L N N X H G L I R I O S S E A C F M A E
I G S C F K K O K Y N Y A U N I T G L G
H I K D X U I C V D O S L D Q D Y N I O
T Z C Q Z P L Q E I J N T Q U I I G V I
D Q P U N I S H M E N T E E G Z E N E D
L P X A E T G L L R H G V D A X H G G D
G O F A Q N S G F G S L U N D D K H O B
U W Z Q C U S G P N E D S K H B E G N H
B B W X S I E J E V E R Y T H I N G D H
S K H E K G X B D U J T O U Y G H O T A
I J J S L S X I X F V P X E M M H Z V Q
N U R C G J A D P G Z B Q X G O O D U D
V S F F T K G N X J F I N D A W O R D C
F W I J K Y V B U L B M C K I Q B V O I
F W L R C F X N Q C M A I W O O K I N D
```

So... what does all this mean for us?

There are really only 2 ways to live

You can say 'No' to God, and keep pretending to be your own king—but God will punish you by shutting you out of his good kingdom forever.

Or you can say 'sorry' to God, start living with Jesus as your king, and enjoy being in God's kingdom forever.

At the start of this book, I said I wanted to ask you a really big question…

Who will be your king?

 Draw yourself under the crown of the king you choose.

1.

ME

2.

JESUS GOD

THE BIBLE SAYS

Everyone who trusts in the Son has eternal life. But everyone who rejects him will never share in that life. (John 3:36)

How can you **start** living with Jesus as your king?

You can talk to God…

You can say to God: Dear God, I'm sorry that I haven't treated you as my king. I'm sorry that I've said 'No' to you by not doing what you say. Thank you for sending Jesus to die on the cross to take away my punishment. Please forgive me, and help me to live with Jesus as my king from now on. Amen.

…say sorry to God for not treating him as your king.

…say thank you to God for sending Jesus to die so that you could be forgiven.

…ask God to please forgive you, and help you to live with Jesus as your king. Because of what Jesus has done for you, God *will* forgive you—he's promised!

So how can you keep living God's way—with Jesus as your king? Three things will help:

Pray

see page 25

Read the Bible

see page 26

Talk to others

see page 28

KEEP GOING ➔

How do you **keep** living with Jesus as your king?

 Talking to God is called 'prayer'. God loves you so much, he wants you to pray to him and he hears you. You can talk to God every day—anywhere and any time.

 Draw an inside and an outside picture.

You can talk to God inside…	You can talk to God outside…

Every day you can say 'Sorry God', 'Thank you God' and 'Please God help me and other people'. You can ask God to keep forgiving you and to help you live with Jesus as your king.

Draw or write in these boxes.

What can you thank God for?

Who can you pray for?

READ THE BIBLE

The Bible is *the most* important book. By reading or listening to the Bible you can learn more about God, King Jesus, and living with Jesus as your king. God made us, so he knows the best way for us to live. In the Bible, God tells us how he wants us to live.

God's book, the Bible, is a very special book. It has lots of little books in it. A good place to start reading the Bible is the book of 'Mark'—it tells us all about Jesus.

This is the name of the book.

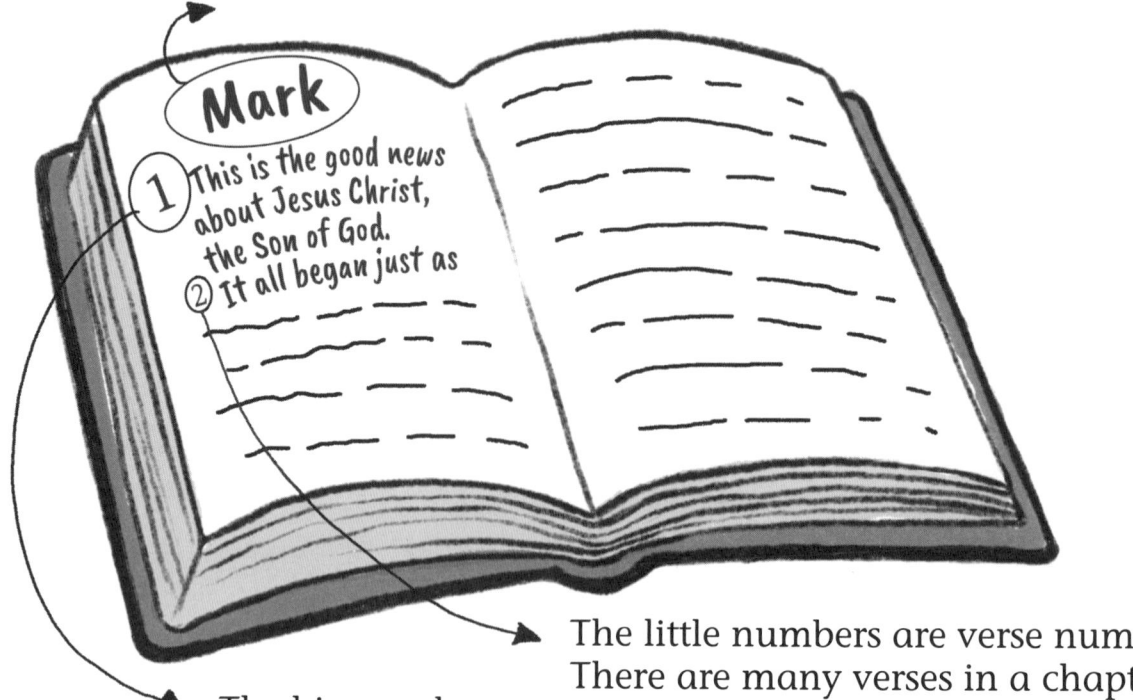

Mark

1 This is the good news about Jesus Christ, the Son of God.
2 It all began just as

The little numbers are verse numbers. There are many verses in a chapter.

The big numbers are chapter numbers. This is chapter 1.

You can also look up Bible verses and read them. Here's one of the Bible verses we've read before. It's Genesis 1:1, which means Genesis chapter 1, verse 1.

THE BIBLE SAYS

In the beginning, God created the heavens and the earth.
(Genesis 1:1)

 There are Bible verses in these treasure chests. You can try to find the verses in a Bible. If you don't have a Bible, they are also written on page 30.

Philippians 2:8

Ephesians 2:8-9

1 John 4:9

1 John 1:9

Romans 5:8

Psalm 145:13

GOOD THINGS TO REMEMBER

1 John 4:11

2 Timothy 3:16

Psalm 118:1

Ephesians 4:31-32

Colossians 4:2

Psalm 86:5

Psalm 89:11

Psalm 145:3

Psalm 147:5

Psalm 145:8

HOW GOD WANTS US TO LIVE

WHAT WE CAN THANK GOD FOR

TALK TO OTHERS

People who live with Jesus as their king are called 'Christians'.

It's important to talk to other Christians who can help you live with Jesus as your king. (Maybe the person who gave you this book?)

A church is a group of Christians. When they meet together each week, they learn more about God and Jesus. They pray and sing. They help each other live with Jesus as their king.

 Here are some people who are part of a church together.
Spot the differences in the two pictures.

There are Christians living all over the world. They all look different. They live in different places. But they will all be together in God's good kingdom forever.

Crossword Puzzle

Let's see how well you can remember what we've learned by doing this crossword puzzle. If you're not sure about the answer for each clue, you can go back and look for it on the page shown at the end of the clue.

ACROSS

3. What people who follow Jesus are called. (10) page 28
5. The Bible gives us this type of news. (4) page 18
6. The person who was punished instead of us. (5) page 17
9. Who God is king of. (8) page 4
11. What we deserve for saying 'No' to God. (10) page 11
12. The name of God's special book. (5) page 2

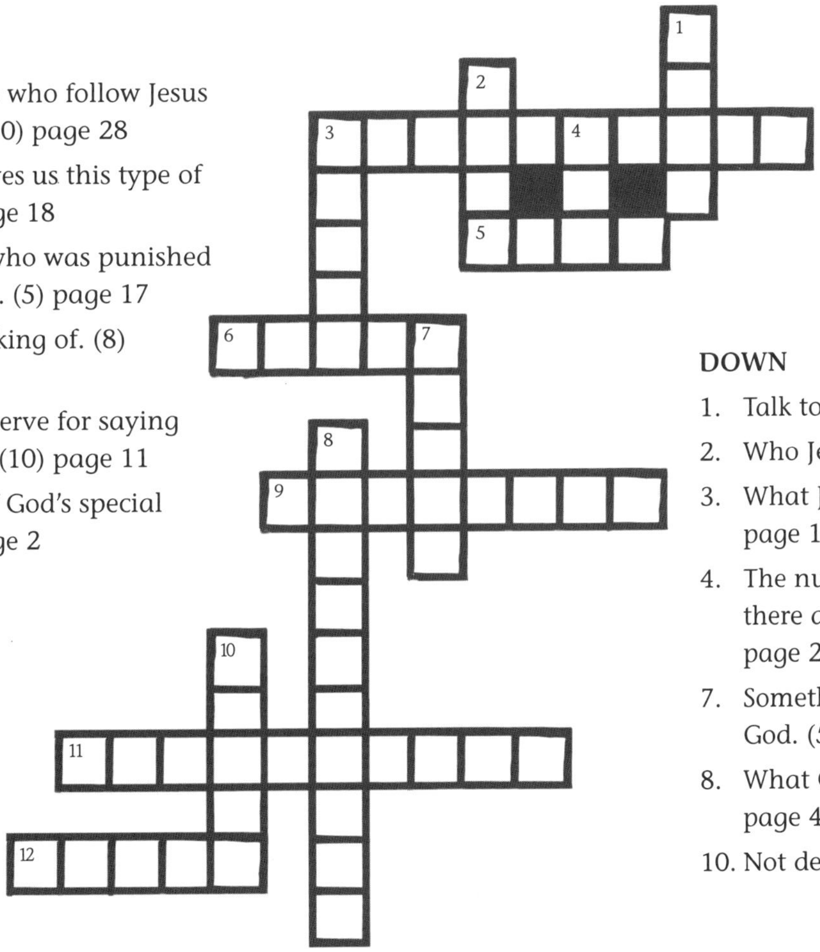

DOWN

1. Talk to God. (4) page 25
2. Who Jesus is. (4) page 19
3. What Jesus died on. (5) page 17
4. The number of ways there are to live. (3) page 23
7. Something we can say to God. (5) page 24
8. What God is king of. (10) page 4
10. Not dead. (5) page 21

It's time to say goodbye. Here's some good news for you to try to remember. It's a Bible verse we read earlier...

God loved the world so much that he gave his only Son, so that everyone who trusts in him will have eternal life. (John 3:16)

Bible Verses

GOOD THINGS TO REMEMBER

Psalm 145:13—Your [God's] kingdom will never end, and you will rule forever. Our Lord, you keep your word and do everything you say.

Romans 5:8—But God showed how much he loved us by having Christ die for us, even though we were sinful.

Ephesians 2:8-9—You were saved by faith in God, who treats us much better than we deserve. This is God's gift to you, and not anything you have done on your own. It isn't something you have earned, so there is nothing you can brag about.

Philippians 2:8—Christ was humble. He obeyed God and even died on a cross.

1 John 1:9—But if we confess our sins to God, he can always be trusted to forgive us and take our sins away.

1 John 4:9—God showed his love for us when he sent his only Son into the world to give us life.

HOW GOD WANTS US TO LIVE

Psalm 118:1—Tell the Lord how thankful you are, because he is kind and always merciful.

Ephesians 4:31-32—Stop being bitter and angry and mad at others. Don't yell at one another or curse each other or ever be rude. Instead, be kind and merciful, and forgive others, just as God forgave you because of Christ.

Colossians 4:2—Never give up praying. And when you pray, keep alert and be thankful.

2 Timothy 3:16—Everything in the Scriptures [the Bible] is God's Word. All of it is useful for teaching and helping people and for correcting them and showing them how to live.

1 John 4:11—Dear friends, since God loved us this much, we must love each other.

WHAT WE CAN THANK GOD FOR

Psalm 86:5—You willingly forgive, and your love is always there for those who pray to you.

Psalm 89:11—The heavens and the earth belong to you. And so does the world with all its people because you created them.

Psalm 145:3—You are wonderful, Lord, and you deserve all praise, because you are much greater than anyone can understand.

Psalm 145:8—You are merciful, Lord! You are kind and patient and always loving.

Psalm 147:5—Our Lord is great and powerful! He understands everything.

Answers

page 6
God is a <u>kind</u>, <u>loving</u> and <u>good</u> king.

page 8 Maze solution —>

page 13 Quick quiz
1. always does the right thing
2. punish us

page 14
- God is the only true —> king.
- God will set up a —> wonderful kingdom.
- God's kingdom will —> never end.
- People who keep saying 'No' to God and keep disobeying him —> can't be in God's kingdom.

page 14
There is GOOD NEWS.

page 22
Jesus is our alive-forever king who can help us.

page 22 Find-a-word —>

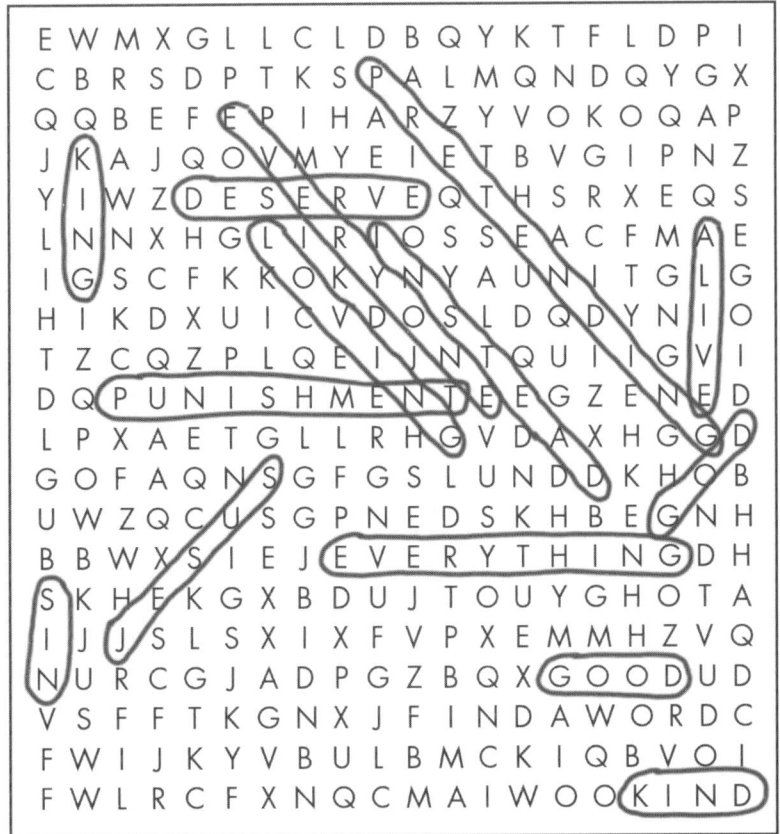

31

page 28 Spot the difference

page 29 Crossword puzzle

ACROSS

3. CHRISTIANS
5. GOOD
6. JESUS
9. EVERYONE
11. PUNISHMENT
12. BIBLE

DOWN

1. PRAY
2. KING
3. CROSS
4. TWO
7. SORRY
8. EVERYTHING
10. ALIVE

Bible Words Dictionary

created (page 4)—made

heavens (page 4)—everything up in the sky

acceptable to God (page 7)—doing what God wants all the time and in every way

turned away (page 7)—saying 'No' to God and not living with him as king

face judgement (page 11)—get what we deserve from God (punishment)

eternal life (page 15)—living in God's wonderful kingdom forever

trusts (page 15)—believes that Jesus is the King and has done everything for us to be forgiven

heaven (page 19)—the special place God lives

tomb (page 20)—a cave where they put Jesus' dead body, blocked off by a huge stone

Lord's angel (page 20)—God's messenger

disciples (page 20)—Jesus' friends